Sabine Pröbstl

Global Innovation. Buzzword or Growth Strategy?

GRIN Verlag

Bibliografische Information der Deutschen Nationalbibliothek:

Die Deutsche Bibliothek verzeichnet diese Publikation in der Deutschen National-
bibliografie; detaillierte bibliografische Daten sind im Internet über http://dnb.d-
nb.de/ abrufbar.

Imprint:

Copyright © 2013 GRIN Verlag GmbH
Druck und Bindung: Books on Demand GmbH, Norderstedt Germany
ISBN: 978-3-656-49263-4

This book at GRIN:

http://www.grin.com/en/e-book/232374/global-innovation-buzzword-or-growth-
strategy

GRIN - Your knowledge has value

Der GRIN Verlag publiziert seit 1998 wissenschaftliche Arbeiten von Studenten, Hochschullehrern und anderen Akademikern als eBook und gedrucktes Buch. Die Verlagswebsite www.grin.com ist die ideale Plattform zur Veröffentlichung von Hausarbeiten, Abschlussarbeiten, wissenschaftlichen Aufsätzen, Dissertationen und Fachbüchern.

Visit us on the internet:

http://www.grin.com/

http://www.facebook.com/grincom

http://www.twitter.com/grin_com

GLOBAL INNOVATION - BUZZWORD OR GROWTH STRATEGY?

Sabine Pröbstl, MBA

Contents

Abstract

This research paper examines the question: Is innovation a critical success factor for today business or merely a modern buzzword? Setting the example of the ITC and luxury goods industry

Europe is increasingly under innovation pressure. Is innovation increasing the profit of firms and the growth strategy of European companies?

Even today there are sharp divisions among experts regarding the definition of innovation.

But they agree that innovation is being something new and expected to risk. When defining something new, the experts can't agree.

Keywords: 3 – 10 innovation, buzzword, growth strategy, swarovski

Introduction

Definition and demarcation of the concept of innovation

Mobilkom Austria and Telekom Austria was merged in 2010 and now form together A1 Telekom Austria. One of the main problems of the company is the management of innovations and to find a clear innovation strategy.

Strategy & Planning is the executive department of CCO Area at A1 Telekom Austria who is assigned to this Project. The main goal is to clear and implement an innovation definition, strategy, process and business unit at A1 Telekom Austria

For further discussion we have to define for ourselves: what is innovation about?

Invention

Invention is a necessary preliminary stage in the process of innovation. It is restricted to the process of knowledge generation through research and development, and the technical realization of a new problem solution for the first time. This can take place in both a planned and an unplanned way.[1] Creative ideas and technical realizations are by no means innovative.

Innovation

The term 'innovation' comes from the Latin *innovatio*, and is translated as follows: Innovation = Lat. *innovatio*, meaning 'introduction', 'renewal', or 'renovation', which can be traced back to *novus* ('new').[2]

An innovation is principally understood as being the commercial application of a new problem solution for the first time. It aims to achieve the introduction to market and market probation ('diffusion') of the invention in the form of a new product or process.

Innovation can be expressed in a formula:

Innovation = Idea + Invention + Diffusion[3]

---

[1] Schlick, G.H. 1995 S. 2
[2] Vahs D., Burmester R. "Innovationsmanagement- Von der Produktidee zur erfolgreichen Vermarktung, 1999
[3] Müller-Prothmann, Nina Dör: „Innovationsmanagement"- 2.Auflage

The difference between this and invention related to a specific point in time is the result of a process or the process itself, which passes through all the stages in the innovation process. From idea generation through to successful diffusion in the market.

Innovation management

Innovation management is an holistic management task which should be sustained above and beyond any hierarchical levels. The basis for innovation management is an innovation culture embedded and lived in the corporate culture, both from the top down and the bottom up.

The tasks of innovation management can be wide-ranging, and vary from company to company. The fundamental principle is management of the innovation process, from idea generation through to successful marketing and the achievement of diffusion. It takes in both strategic and operational tasks.

The aims of innovation management can be divided up at three levels:

- The nominative level, such as the vision, mission, values and overall concepts
- The strategic level, such as resources, technologies, knowledge and competences of employees, markets, customers, suppliers, cooperation partners and competitors
- The operational level, such as the design and management of the innovation process, service, quality, costs and time[4]

Differentiation of innovation types

Innovations can be classified in different categories based on various criteria and features. Possible criteria and features for the differentiation of innovations: field of enquiry, trigger, level of novelty and scope of change. There are, of course, other differentiating features for innovations.

Important for A1 Telekom Austria are the product innovations and process innovations and the connection between the innovation types.

---

[4] Gassmann O., "Innovation- Zufall oder Management?", München 2008

Product innovation

Products are material and immaterial services provided in the market by a company which are suited to satisfying the customer's needs thanks to specific features. A product consists of its product core, the product exterior, and the additional services. The product core consists of the technical-constructive features and basic functions, while the product exterior allows for a wide range of variations. The extent to which a company is able to develop the Unique Selling Point (USP) and product benefits into an unmistakable product personality is crucial for the product.

Product innovations are of particularly high economic importance for a company. Increasing and changing customer needs lead to ever-shorter product life cycles, and thereby to a wide and diverse product range in the market. The basic aim of product innovation, therefore, is for a company to defend its competitive position through market introduction and to satisfy the wishes of its customers. [5]

"Surveys show that product innovations are associated with a considerable risk of failure. Of every 100 product ideas, just 3.7 percent actually make it as successes in the market. Another survey shows that of every 58 product ideas in the USA, just one could be successfully implemented in the market." (cf. Nieschlag, R/ Dichtl, E/ Hörschgen, H 1997, p. 262).

Despite this, product innovations are the highest form of the innovation stages. While they are highly risky and cost-intensive, successful innovations increase competitive advantages, and structured innovation management increases the opportunities for economic success.

Process innovation

A process is understood as the targeted provision of a service by means of a sequence of activities. The service is provided in a certain order, a certain processing time, and according to certain rules. Process innovations can also be described as 'process innovation'.

Pleschak/Sabisch criticise the fact that process innovations are paid relatively little attention.

The internal efficiency of the company is only of interest to the customer him- or herself if it has an impact on the quality of the product. A balance should be struck between product and

---

[5] Vahs D. Innovationsarten, 1999 S. 72- 76

process innovations at any company in order to create appropriate competitive advantage in the market.[6]

Connection between product and process innovations

So when should a company press ahead with processes, and when with product innovations? Harvard Professors J. Abernathy and James M. Utterback explored this question. The results of empirical surveys show that the manufacturing process is becoming increasingly important. The scope for further improvements to be made in the course of the product lifecycle is becoming narrower. The fact is, however, that while product innovations are an important driver of growth, improving the manufacturing process in order to achieve financial success is more valuable still. The progress in research reduces as a product ages. Both recommend, therefore, concentrating on improving processes as certain products become older, so yields can continue to be increased. [7]

The changing of sides does not happen entirely voluntarily, however: low-cost providers exert massive pressure on the market. Not all customers are interested in innovative products; instead, they are looking for cheap offers and rates, as shown by the latest results of an empirical survey carried out in the telecommunications environment.[8]

Diagram 1: Connection between product and process innovations

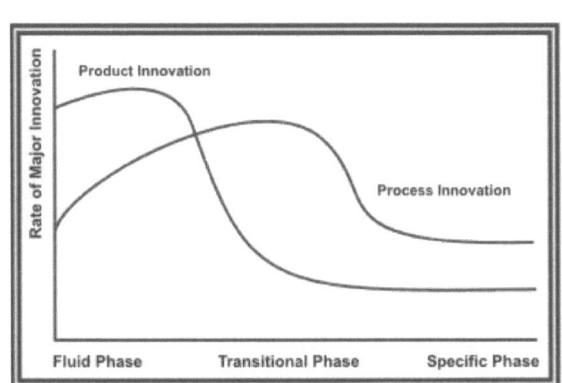

[6] Pleschak F./ Sabisch H. 1996 , S.20
[7] Scheuss R „Handbuch der Strategien" 2012, S.262- 265
[8] Brand Tracking A1, „Was verstehen Sie unter Innovation?'"", 2012

Innovation strategies

The management and control of innovation, growth fields is a major challenge. The main strategies and models found in subsequent chapters

S-curve product & innovation improvement

Originally developed in mathematics, the S-curve was later adopted in fields such as political economy and innovation research. It is a scientific tool used for depicting development processes. S-curves are helpful for illustrating innovative cycles to determine exactly which stage of development the respective technology has reached at a particular time.

Arthur D. Little has developed a classification of innovation dynamics:

- Pace setter technologies: although still under development and highly risky, these have the necessary potential to stir up the area of business.
- Key technologies: influence the contemporary competitive situation of the company in the long term. These are the supporter of progress.
- Basic technologies: when technologies become basic technologies, they have lost their differentiating feature, and are used by most providers.[9]

Diagram 3: The Innovation S-Curve, UTB School of Business, Dr Kroll

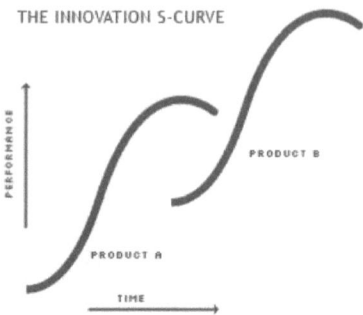

---

[9] Scheuss R. „Handbuch der Strategien", 2012 S.262

Kondratiev Cycles

Nikolai Kondratiev, who published his theory of cyclical economic development – "The Major Cycles of the Conjuncture" – in 1926. The economist established that fluctuations in the economic cycle overlapped with large, long wave movements. These waves lasted approximately 30-60 years, and showed similar patterns. He recognized important discoveries and developments in the 'upswing wave', which drive these positive dynamics, and which he named 'basic innovations'. Each new cycle begins with dissatisfaction with existing solutions on the part of consumers. This leads to the rethinking of, and searching for, new solutions for existing technologies.[10]

Diagram 4: Kondratiev Cycles

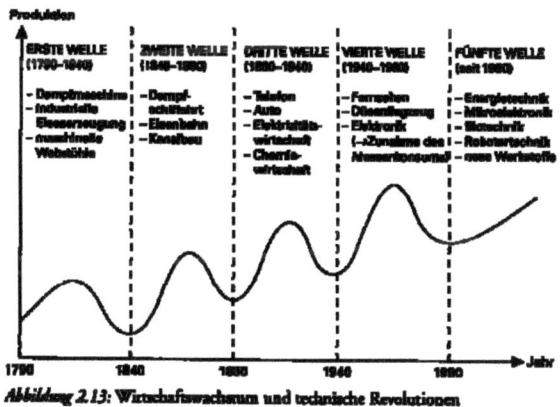

Abbildung 2.13: Wirtschaftswachstum und technische Revolutionen

Hype Cycle

Every technology goes through a Hype Cycle at its introduction. Jackie Fenn[11] (vgl. Diagram 5), a consultant for the IT research company, has investigated this dynamic: the 'hype' should be understood as the bow-wave of interest which swells innovations into an inordinately large wave by strengthening the media and society. The bases for other innovations can also be laid here.

---

[10] Vahs D. „Innovationsmanagement" 1999, S5-8
[11] Scheuss R. „Handbuch der Strategien", 2012 S 255

Diagram 5: Hype Cycle for Consumer Technologies, 2007 [12]

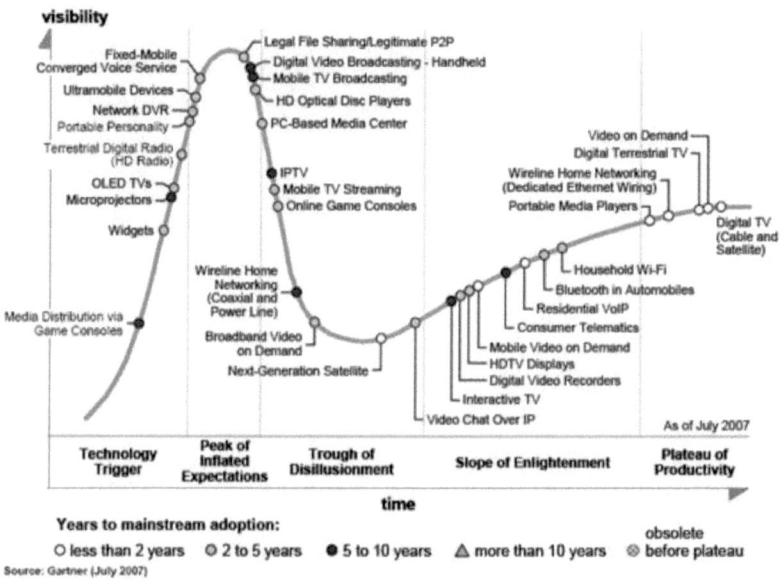

The hype cycle is an important aspect of management. Strategic evaluation of an innovation is extremely difficult – although the bow-wave of the hype cycle is tough to interpret in any event. Decision-makers in the field have been confronted with the dilemma that they must either miss out on important trends or make investments that are far too early and involve too much risk.

Important for A1 Telekom is the Innovation Strategy and the question: Incremental or radical innovations for shaping the future? Now, there is just incremental innovation strategy- but is it the right one?

[12] Gartner Hype Cycle, http://www.gartner.com/technology/innovation/

Incremental & radical innovation

'Incremental innovation' means improving product or business processes in small steps. Incremental innovation strategies can be found at most companies. In many cases, this strategy is described as a "step-by-step, spontaneous process of muddling through". Experts agree that this form of improvement is not sufficient to gain an advantage in the market and in competition. If you want to establish yourself as an innovation pioneer, a higher innovation dynamic is necessary. In many cases, hierarchical barriers within a company are an inconvenience. Innovations require creativity, an enjoyment of experimentation and spontaneous forms of organization.[13]

Radical innovations are not content with small, logical improvements to incremental innovations. Radical innovators are searching for leaps or breaks. Their content consists of new product lines, opening up new markets, making dramatic improvements in business processes, and new business models. At the same time, radical innovations are fraught with risk and tricky, and the flop rate is very high. The challenge with radical innovations is to grant the necessary resources for the innovation project over an extended period of time, even though no revenues are expected in the short term. What is beyond question is that radical innovations offer the greater chance for companies to shift the competitive position in their own favor.[14]

---

[13] Vahs D. „Innovationsmanagement" 1999, S5-10
[14] Scheuss R. "Handbuch der Strategien" 2012, S.257-260

The table below contrasts incremental innovation strategy with radical innovation strategy.

	Incremental innovation strategy	Radical innovation strategy
Focus	Short-term view over 6,12 or 24 months; focus on improving product and costs	Longer-term; view over the coming 5-10 years; focus on new product development, new business processes, and new business modeling
Course, certainty	Familiar, continuous, logical, low level of uncertainty	Unfamiliar, dramatic, high level of uncertainty, fragmentary
Relationship to business	Development related to existing business model in order to remain up-to-date	Development related to still unfamiliar business model being developed in order to improve competitive/market position
Organization	Rooted in existing organization, formal process	Key developers come and go, across different sectors, internal and external, project organization
Resources	Focuses on familiar knowledge and uses familiar approaches	Develops learning processes, builds on new skills, develops new types of resource
Modeling	In small steps	In (major) leaps

Diagram 6: Types of innovation[15]

Levels of technological and market-side change tend to be low in the telecommunications sector. As a result, the focus on incremental innovation is well-established at most companies. The telecommunications market in Austria is one of the most intensely competitive in Europe. Customer needs focusing on cheap offers limit the power of domestic telecommunications providers to innovate.

---

[15] Scheuss Ralph „Innovationsmuster- handbuch der Strategien" 2012, S 258

Level of market and technological change in telecommunications

Diagram 7: Level of innovation

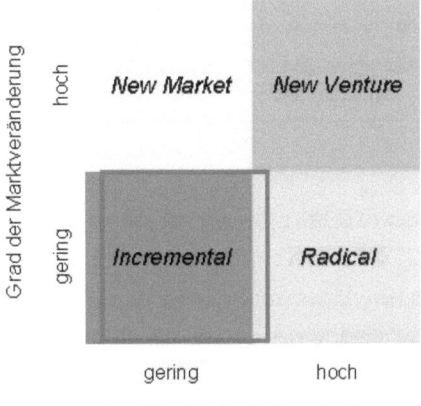

At the beginning of this century, Harvard Professor and Austrian national economist Joseph Alois Schumpeter defined innovations as the "implementation of new combinations". According to his theory, it is only the "creative destructive power" of an innovative activity which takes place not incrementally but intermittently that drives economic development forward.[16]

All development builds upon creative destruction, as old structures founder in order to make space for new ones. Pioneers bear the force both of destruction and of creative renewal. These innovations are effective in removing old-fashioned solutions and in breaking up new, inefficient structures. According to Schumpeter's theory, innovations are in fact the engine of economic development.

Understanding of innovation in the telecommunications customer survey

The empirical part of this paper deals with the issue of the "Understanding of Innovation" from the customer's viewpoint, which was drawn up as part of the A1 Brand Tracking by the

---

[16] Schumpeter, J.A 1987 S.100

operator A1 Telekom Austria. This shows a differentiated picture of the understanding of innovation in the telecommunications industry.

Key points in the survey:

- Most important subjects associated with innovative telecommunications providers: good, new and cheap offers, and rates harmonized with customers' needs

- Consumers do not associate technology as being an issue of the greatest importance here

- A1 and Drei are viewed as being the most innovative relative to their competitors – which is interesting above all in connection with A1 as a premium (as opposed to 'cheap') provider. Here, the evaluation is obviously influenced first and foremost by the large number of offers, as well as by the image advantage as a technological and quality-related leader, and market leadership. [17]

The understanding of innovation amongst customers affects the range and rates above all. The various low-cost providers in this market environment, which satisfy the customer's need for cheap offers and rates, mean the environment for product innovations is a difficult one.

Diagram 2: Brand tracking/study results

Die wichtigsten Themen in Zusammenhang mit einem innovativen Telco Anbieter

Best practice: Swarovski

The picture is a different one in the luxury goods industry. This chapter deals with a corporate analysis of an Austrian operator in the luxury goods industry which has established itself very successfully as an innovator in the market. Innovation management is one of a number of key policies to be drawn up and lived at Swarovski.

The Case Study is based on Interviews with employees, senior management of Swarovski and Website research.

About Swarovski

Founded in 1895 by Daniel Albert Swarovski, the Austrian company Swarovski today is the world's leading producer for cut crystal.

Swarovski Group employs approximately 31.458 people, owns 1.280 boutiques and have 1200 partner boutiques. The Retail Network reached worldwide 42 countries and have production sites in 8 countries: China, Indien, Jordanien, Liechtenstein, Österreich, Thailand, Tschechische Republik, USA[18]

A basic prerequisite for the leadership in the world market is the launch of innovative products and services as well as the further development of a strong brand. In order to survive in a fast changing market environment, Swarovski restructured their innovation management during the last few years.[19]

Innovation at Swarovski works as follows:

The INNOnetwork at Swarovski includes three main components:

- The i-flash community, an IT-based tool
- The i-LAB
- The "Steuerungsgruppe"

---

[18] http://www.brand.swarovski.com/Content.Node/aboutus/factsfigures/RZ-FACTSHEET-DE-SWAcorp_ONLINE.pdf
[19] Erler H., Vice President Innovation at Swarovski

The central element of the innovation management of Swarovski is the idea community called "i-flash". It is a platform and an interface and encourages employees to contribute with their creativity to the innovation activities of the company. In order to integrate the various innovation activities, Swarovski implemented a proper organizational entity, the so-called "i-LAB". The i-LAB built up a deep understanding of the needs and wishes of the various business units and now coordinates the communication between different levels and departments. It comprises a process with all the stages of the innovation process, especially in the front-end area, from idea generation and idea selection to prototype visualization. Commercialization areas (Product Development, Production, Marketing, Sales) are represented within the steering group of the INNOnetwork, but are not an explicit part of the i-LAB.[20]

The i-LAB is a team of eight people offering support, handling and management of ideas submitted to the i-flash software by employees. On the basis of strategic criteria, the i-LAB team performs a first screen of an idea and then further develops, enriches and enhances the idea. At this point, the enriched ideas are put into i-flash again to be sent to key players in the company for a precise evaluation and for supporting comments and suggestions. With this feedback, the i-LAB creates a full concept of the idea, which is then presented to Gate 1 in the corresponding business unit in Swarovski's Stage-Gate process.

The criteria for the idea selection are based on the following three points:

• A business unit believes in an idea and immediately takes it into their development roadmap.
• The i-LAB believes in an idea. Due to the advice and the remarks from the evaluation process, i-LAB invests in closer evaluation and further development as well as in the visualization with a prototype.
• General criteria for the evaluation are gut feeling, new to market, new to company, potential of the idea, possible growth, strategic and technological fit. [21]

Two or three times a year, representatives from the core areas for innovation, i.e. F&E, product development and marketing, are invited to events from the INNOnetwork. Irrespective of the business unit or hierarchical level, the participants discuss future trends, incremental improvements and radical future ideas on the basis of strategic fields. The so

---

[20] Erler H, Vice President Innovation at Swarovski
[21] Erler H, "Swarovski Innovation Elements" Slide 7

called "Steuerungsgruppe", consisting of decision makers from research, production and product development, takes over the management of the ideas emerged from those meetings. The meetings offered the possibility for the innovation manager of the business units to inform each other about the ongoing innovation activities in each unit. The result was six aligned innovation topics the managers agreed on. In order to assure that the innovation process complies with the actual business requirements, the "Steuerungsgruppe" checks ideas and innovations for benefits and feasibility.[22]

Swarovski's success factors

- Soft leadership through the creation of the ideal surroundings for innovative and effective activities.
- Communication of company values through visions and mission statements.
- Strong entrepreneurship-culture to support ideas and innovations as a basic condition.
- Emotional culture of a family business shaping employees' attitude.
- Employees are considered an unlimited source of good ideas and get the possibility to evaluate and further develop their ideas.
- Communication of importance of innovation and dedication of proper resources to innovation, also in difficult times.
- Open network of information, communication and production to connect people and knowledge.
- Combination of top-down and bottom-up approach in order to enhance commitment.
- Communication between the business units (Erler, Wilhelmer; Cooper, Edgett).[23]

---

[22] Based on Interview with Management and employees at Swarovski
[23] Based on Interviews with Erler

Comparison A1 Telekom Austria and Swarovski

A1 Telekom Austria AG	*Swarovski AG*
Organisation	
The Inno Broker Concept	*I-Lab, INNOnetwork*
The A1 Local Innovation Team is the virtual network to identify and co-ordinate innovation activities. Representatives from the fields of CTO, CCO and CEO. No Central Business Unit and Full Time FTE's[24]	The INNOnetwork is the virtual network for Innovation activities. Representatives from the fields CTO, CCO and CEO Cross-functional business unit with defined processes and innovation tools. - The I-Lab Core Team - The "Steuerungsgruppe"[25]
Strategy	
Leading Innovation in the Growth	With a nod to the past…

---

[24] St.Hauer, „Innovationskultur", Workshop A1 Telekom Austria- Results, 2011, F. 8
[25] H. Erler, Vice President Innovation- Swarovski, 2010 F. 7

fields:	...and a laser eye to the future.
Cloud Services	An epic with no end.
Unified Communications	
Mobile Payment[26]	
Definition	
At now, there is no clear definition what is Innovation about. The Project for Implement and clear the definition of Innovation is ongoing.[27]	**INNOVATION = A new business concept that can foster significant and sustainable top-line growth.** • Successful innovations must: • Differentiate the brand • Occur fast enough to stay ahead of competition • Occur often enough to keep our brand relevant[28]

Conclusion & recommendation: does innovation increase profit?

Because the level of change in the technological and market-side regards is minimal in the telecommunications industry in Austria, it is not advisable for the company A1 Telekom to adopt an exclusively incremental innovation strategy. The focus should be on product innovations which achieve a substantial leap forward and competitive advantage, and consequently on a strategy of radical innovation. In the longer term, the current vision for achieving and defending innovation leadership can be achieved with an exclusively incremental strategy, and small improvements alone.

According to evaluations of interviews and the customer survey in the telecommunications environment, structured innovation management is becoming increasingly important at the company A1Telekom, first and foremost in product innovations.

Innovations are a lever for lasting commercial success. Whilst the flop rate of product innovations may be high, this risk can be reduced by structured innovation management, so increasing the chances of commercial success.

---

[26] Strategy Paper 2012, Strategy & Planning CCO Area
[27] Management Board A1 Telekom Austria, 2012
[28] Strategy Paper, Swarovski, 2012

References

Vahs Dietmar/ Burmester R, (1999), "Innovationsmanagement" Definition und Abgrenzung des Innovationsbegriffs 2, 41-44.

Müller-Prothmann, Nina Dör(2011): „Innovationsmanagement"- 2.Auflage S7-12

Hartschen M./ Scherer J. (2009): „Innovationsmanagement- Die 6 Phasen von der Idee zur Umsetzung"- S. 7

Scheuss R. (2012): „Handbuch der Strategien, 220 Konzepte der Weltbeten Vordenker" S. 246- 283

Nieschlag, R/ Dichtl, E/ Hörschgen, (1997) „Marketing" S. 262

Gassmann O.(2008) "Innovation- Zufall oder Management?", München S 1-23

Schumpeter, J.A (1987) „Theorie der wirtschaftlichen Entwicklung" S.100

Pleschak F./ Sabisch H (1996) „Innovationsmanagement"

Internal Information and Experts:

Hannes Erler, Vice President Innovation Swarovski

Marco Harfmann, Bereichsleiter Residential & Small Business Marketing

Alfred Mahringer, Bereichsleitung KVP & PMO

Dr. Hannes Ametsreiter, CEO A1 Telekom Austria

Alexander Sperl, CCO A1 Telekom Austria AG

Innovation in the Telecom Industry, Quantitative Analyse:

Erhebungszeitraum: 21.05.2012 – 27.05.2012,

W-based User: 502 ab 14 Jahren